◆ LET'S EXPLORE SCIENCE ○

Make it Change

▲ David Evans and Claudette Williams □

Scholastic Canada Ltd

A DORLING KINDERSLEY BOOK

Project Editor Dawn Sirett
Art Editor Karen Fielding
Managing Editor Jane Yorke
Managing Art Editor Chris Scollen
Production Jayne Wood
Photography by Susanna Price

First published in Great Britain in 1992
by Dorling Kindersley Limited,
9 Henrietta Street, London WC2E 8PS

Published in Canada in 1992
by Scholastic Canada Ltd.,
123 Newkirk Road, Richmond Hill, Ontario,
Canada L4C 3G5

Canadian Cataloguing in Publication Data
Evans, David, 1937-
Make it change
(Let's explore science)
Includes index.
ISBN 0-590-74511-5
1. Change of state (Physics) – Juvenile literature.
2. Change of state Physics) – Experiments –
Juvenile literature. I. Williams, Claudette.
II. Title. III. Series: Let's explore science
(Richmond Hill, Ont.).
QC301.E83 1992   j541.3   C92-094427-2

Reproduced by J. Film Process Singapore Pte., Ltd.
Printed and bound in Belgium by Proost

Dorling Kindersley would like to thank the following for their help in
producing this book: Steve Shott (for additional photography); Coral Mula
(for safety symbol artwork); Yael Freudmann; Monica Byles; Mark
Richards; Roger Priddy; Chris Legee; Rowena Alsey; Jane Coney; Jenny
Vaughan; and the Futcher School, Drayton, Portsmouth. Dorling
Kindersley would also like to give special thanks to the following for
appearing in this book: Natalie Agada; Heidi Barnes; Hannah Capleton;
Laura Dockrill; Karen Edwards; Leigh Hamilton; William Lindsay; Tony
Locke; Gemma Loke; Rachael Malicki; Chloe O'Connor; Tebedge Ricketts;
Hugo Sandys; Jay Sprake; John Walden; and Jack Winer.

Contents

Note to parents and teachers

Young children are forever asking questions about the things they see, touch, hear, smell, and taste. The **Let's Explore Science** series aims to foster children's natural curiosity, and encourages them to use their senses to find out about science. Each book features a variety of experiments based on one topic, which draw on a young child's everyday experiences. By investigating familiar activities, such as bouncing a ball, making cakes, or clapping hands, young children will learn that science plays an important part in the world around them.

Investigative approach

Young children can only begin to understand science if they are stimulated to think and to find out for themselves. For these reasons, an open-ended questioning approach is used in the **Let's Explore Science** books and, wherever possible, results of experiments are not shown. Children are encouraged to make their own scientific discoveries, and to interpret them according to their own ideas. This investigative approach to learning makes science exciting and not just about acquiring "facts." It will assist children in many areas of their education.

Using the books

Before starting an experiment, check the text and pictures to ensure that you have gathered any necessary equipment. Allow children to help in this process and to suggest materials to use. Once ready, it is important to let children decide how to carry out the experiment and what the result means to them. You can help by asking questions, such as "What do you think will happen?" or "What did you do?"

Household equipment

All the experiments can be carried out easily at home. In most cases, inexpensive household objects and materials are used.

Guide to experiments

The *Guide to experiments* on pages 28-29 is intended to help parents, teachers, or helpers using this book with children. It gives an outline of the scientific principles underlying the experiments, includes useful tips for carrying out the activities, suggests alternative equipment to use, and additional activities to try.

Safe experimenting

This symbol appears next to experiments where children may require adult supervision or assistance, such as when they are heating things or using sharp tools.

About this book

Make it Change enables children to experiment with a range of materials and substances and to discover various ways to make them change, including heating, cooling, stirring, staining, and

soaking. Children will observe that changes can happen slowly or quickly, and that some changes can be reversed, while others are irreversible.

The experiments draw children's attention to processes that cause change in their immediate environment and that are part of everyday events, such as:

- dissolving, e.g., when sugar forms a solution with hot water;

- freezing, e.g., when water loses heat and forms ice;

- decaying, e.g., when mold grows on a piece of bread;

- evaporation, e.g., when clothes dry on a clothesline.

All of these processes involve the conversion of energy. By working through the activities in **Make it Change**, children will begin to form ideas about these different processes, and to appreciate that "change" doesn't just happen, but always results from physical or chemical interactions.

With your help, young children will enjoy exploring the world of science and discover that finding out is fun.

David Evans and Claudette Williams

Does it change?

Try these experiments and see if things change.

Popsicle
Put a popsicle on your hand. What happens? What happens to a popsicle when you suck it? How does your tongue feel?

Chocolate
Hold some chocolate in your hand. Put some in your mouth. Does the chocolate change?

Butter
Does butter change when you hold it?

Rubbing things
Try rubbing your hands
on some paper or a towel.
How do your hands feel?

Warm drink
Hold your
hand over a
warm drink. What
change do you feel?

Rubbing hands
Rub your hands
together very
quickly. What
happens to
your hands?

Bread
What does bread taste like
when you chew it for a long time?

Does it change in water?

Can you make things change
when you add them to water?

Water experiments
Try putting some
of these things in
water. Do you
see any changes?

What happens if
you stir the water?

vegetable oil

flour

pasta

coffee

salt

toothpaste

sugar

laundry
detergent

Cold and warm water

Try adding these things to cold water. What happens? Now drop them into warm water. Do they change?

ice

butter

tea bag

salty water

powdered paint

Salty water

Stir a lot of salt into warm water until the water turns cloudy. Pour some of the salty water onto a plate. Leave it in a warm place for a long time.

What happens to the salty water? Try this experiment using powdered paint. What happens?

Can you make bubbles?

What happens when you mix dish-washing liquid with water?

Blowing bubbles
Twist together some pipe cleaners to make a bubble blower. Dip it in the bubble mixture. Can you blow bubbles?

Touching bubbles
Can you put your finger inside a bubble without popping it?

Looking at bubbles

Look closely at a bubble. What changes do you see? Can you tell when a bubble is going to pop?

Using your hands

Can you blow a really big bubble using your hands?

Changing bubble blowers

What happens to the bubbles if you change the shape of the bubble blower?

15

Can you stir it?

Do things change when you stir or shake them?

Cornstarch
Add a little milk to some cornstarch. Is it easy to stir? Put the cornstarch aside for a long time. How easy is it to stir now?

Butter
Put some butter in a bowl. Is it easy to stir? Does it change?

Bubble bath
Stir some bubble bath into a bowl of water. What happens?

Egg
Whisk the white part of an egg for a long time. Does it change? What happens if you turn the bowl upside down?

Cream

Pour some cream into a clean jar and screw on the lid. Shake it for a long time. What happens?

Syrup

Stir some syrup. What is it like? Put it in the fridge for a long time. Now stir the syrup again. Has it changed?

Tomato ketchup

What happens when you turn a bottle of ketchup upside down? Now try again, but shake the bottle first. Is there any change?

Can you cook it?

Does food change when you heat or cool it? Ask an adult to help you with these experiments.

Cookies

Make cookie dough (see the recipe on page 29). Cut out thick and thin cookies. Ask an adult to bake them. How do the cookies change?

Raw egg

Crack open a raw egg. What is it like inside?

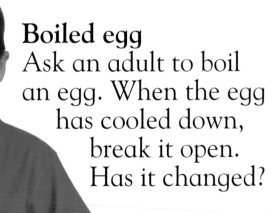

Boiled egg

Ask an adult to boil an egg. When the egg has cooled down, break it open. Has it changed?

Water

Fill a large, plastic tub or an ice tray with water. Put it in the freezer. What happens to the water?

bread

strawberry

Fruit and bread

Leave some fruit or bread in the freezer overnight. Does it change?

Chocolate

Ask an adult to melt some chocolate. Pour the runny chocolate into a dish. Put the dish in the fridge. Does the chocolate change?

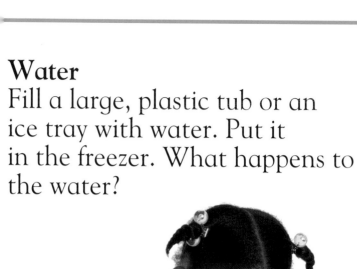

Ice cream

What happens to ice cream when you leave it out of the freezer?

Can you make it wet?

How do things change when
you get them wet?

Wet hands
How do your hands
feel when you put
them in water?

Dry hands
How many ways can
you find to dry your
wet hands? How do
they feel if you blow
on them?

Wet hair
How does your
hair change when
you get it wet?

Dry hair
What happens
when you use a
hair dryer on wet hair?

Wet things

Put some things in water. How do they change?
Which things soak up the most water?

cardboard

sock

washcloth

plastic
apron

pot
holder

Dry things

Hang the things
on a line to dry.
Which ones dry
first? How can
you make the
things dry faster?
Do they look or
feel different
when they are dry?

Can you make it dirty?

What can you use to make a rag dirty?
Can you make the rag clean again?

Making rags
Tear up an old
sheet or some
old clothes
into rags.

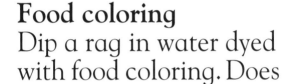

Food coloring
Dip a rag in water dyed
with food coloring. Does
the rag change?

Beets
 Put a rag into a pan
with some water and
sliced beets. Ask an adult
to boil the rag for 15
minutes. What happens?

Mud
Does a rag change
if you rub it in mud?

Washing in water

Can you find a way to clean the dirty rags? Try washing them in water. Does warm water clean better than cold?

Washing in soapy water

Try cleaning the dirty rags with powdered laundry detergent, a bar of soap, or liquid detergent. Which one cleans the best?

Washing stains

Which stains are the hardest to wash out?

Will it change?

Find out if things change when you leave them in soil, in water, or in a warm place.

flags showing the things you have buried

In soil

What will happen if you bury things in the ground or in a pot of earth? If you use a pot or trough, make sure it has holes in the bottom and put it outside on some soil. Water the things you bury and leave them alone for three weeks.

seeds

bolts

lettuce

lettuce in a plastic bag

Look and draw

Draw the items before you bury them. Look at them again when you dig them up. Draw what you see. Have the items changed?

beans

banana

dried fruit

In a saucer of water

Ask an adult to cut off the top of a pineapple or carrot. Put the top in a saucer of water and leave it in a warm place. What happens?

In a jar of water

Do these things change when you soak them in water for a long time?

In a warm place

What happens when you leave bread or fruit in a warm place for a long time?

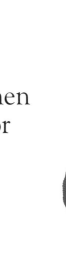

orange

bread

lemon

Look closer

How does the bread change? Try looking at it through a magnifying glass. Now wash your hands.

25

Can you see it change?

Try these experiments. What changes do you see?

Lemon juice

Draw a picture with your finger, using lemon juice as ink. Let the lemon juice dry. Ask an adult to iron your picture. How does it change?

Mirror

What happens if you breathe out close to a mirror? Now try drawing a picture on the mirror using just your finger.

Grape

What happens when you drop a grape into a carbonated drink?

Sugar

Add some sugar to a carbonated drink. How does the drink change?

Fruit and juice

 Half fill a clean plastic cup with strawberries. Pour in some juice. Ask an adult to push a clean popsicle stick through the cup's lid. Put the lid on the cup and leave it in the freezer overnight. What happens?

Index

Guide to experiments

The notes below briefly outline the scientific principles underlying the experiments and include suggestions for alternative equipment to use and activities to try.

Does it change? 10-11

These activities produce changes that children can see, feel, or taste. The bread should be chewed for about a minute (carrot or apple are good alternatives to try).

Does it change in water? 12-13

Dissolving occurs when some substances change when placed in a liquid. Use bouillon cubes or gelatin as alternatives in the water experiments. A saturated salt solution forms crystals when left in a warm place where water can evaporate. (Leave it for about three days.)

Can you make bubbles? 14-15

Adding dish-washing liquid to water makes the water's "skin" more stretchy, enabling bubbles to form. Use a mild solution of dish-washing liquid.

Can you stir it? 16-17

The properties of materials can be changed when energy is applied to them by stirring or shaking. After stirring the cornstarch, leave it for five minutes before stirring it again. Whisk the egg white for about ten minutes. Cream changes after it has been shaken for about ten minutes. To produce a buttery substance, shake the cream for an hour.

Can you cook it? 18-19

The properties of materials can be made to change when they are mixed, cooked, cooled, or frozen.

Gingerbread Men Recipe: Heat the oven to 325°F (170°C). Sift 2 cups (275g) plain flour, 2 teaspoons ground ginger, and 1 teaspoon baking powder into a bowl. Stir in ¹/₂ cup (100g) brown sugar. Cut 6 tablespoons (75g) butter into the flour. Rub the flour and butter between your fingers until it resembles breadcrumbs. Add a beaten egg mixed with ¹/₄ cup (50g) corn syrup and mix everything together well. Knead and roll out the dough. Cut out the cookies and bake them for 15 minutes.

Can you make it wet? 20-21

Some materials change when they are wet. For instance, some shrink. To show various changes, use different materials, such as plastic or paper.

Can you make it dirty? 22-23

Some materials will change color when they are temporarily or permanently stained. Use tea or juice as alternative staining agents.

Will it change? 24-25

Some things change permanently, or decay, when they are buried, left in water, or exposed to air. To show the formation of rust, bury non-galvanized bolts. Leave bread or fruit for a few days to grow mold. Cover decaying food with plastic wrap to prevent children from inhaling fungal or bacterial spores.

Can you see it change? 26-27

Here materials are made to change or behave differently. The lemon juice is heated and becomes visible. When warm air hits the cold mirror, the water vapor in the air condenses, forming tiny water droplets. When the grape is dropped into the soft drink, bubbles stick to the grape, making it buoyant. But when the grape hits the surface of the drink, the bubbles burst and it sinks. This process then repeats. When sugar is added to the soft drink, the drink fizzes because bubbles form on the surface provided by the sugar. The fruit and juice is frozen.

29

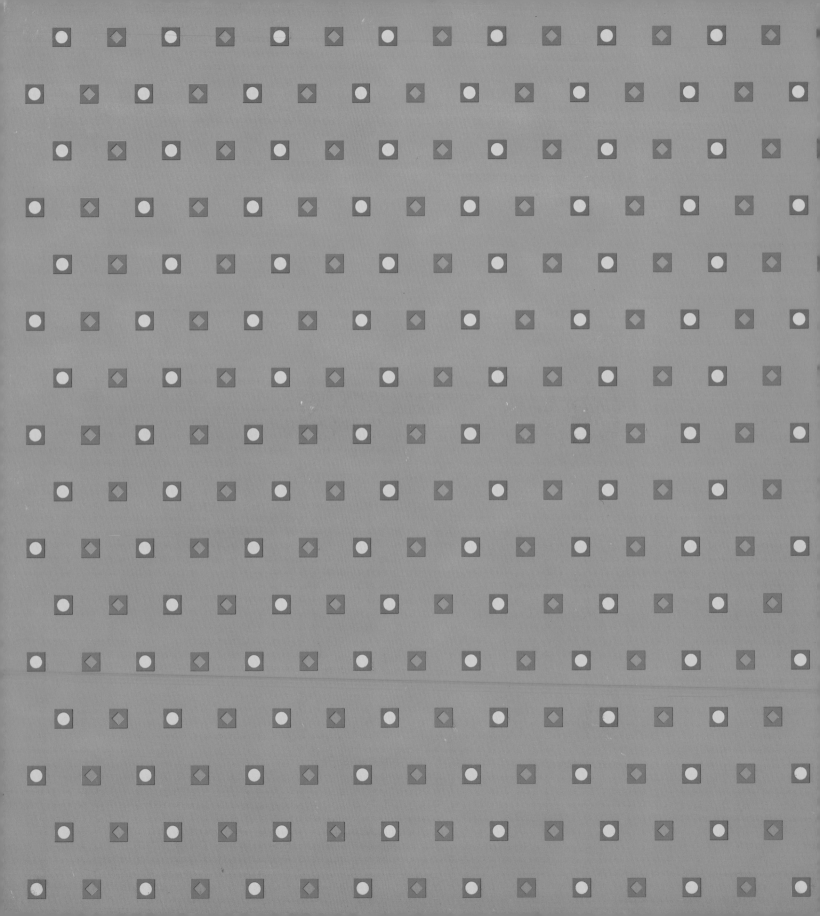